Somewhere to Run From

"We begin with a setting, somewhere to run from."
— Ariel Gore, from *Atlas of the Human Heart*

Somewhere to Run From

Poems

By Tara-Michelle Ziniuk

Tightrope Books Inc.
2009

Copyright © Tara-Michelle Zinuik, 2009

ALL RIGHTS RESERVED. No part of this publication may be reproduced, stored in a retrieval system or transmitted, in any form or by any means, without prior permission of the publisher or, in the case of photocopying or other reprographic copying, a licence from Access Copyright, the Canadian Copyright Licensing Agency, www.accesscopyright.ca, info@accesscopyright.ca.

Tightrope Books
17 Greyton Crescent
Toronto, Ontario
Canada m6e 2g1
www.tightropebooks.com

Canada Council for the Arts / Conseil des Arts du Canada

editor: Sarah Liss
copy editor: Kate Morris
cover design: Romy Ceppetelli
author photo: Shannon Taylor
typesetting: David Bigham

Produced with the support of the Canada Council for the Arts, the Ontario Arts Council and the City of Toronto through the Toronto Arts Council.

Printed in Canada

Library and Archives Canada Cataloguing in Publication

Zinuik, Tara-Michelle
    Somewhere to run from / Tara-Michelle Zinuik.

Poems.
ISBN 978-0-9783351-8-2

    I. Title.
PS8649.I54S66 2009   C811'.6   C2009-901479-3

For Rosa Ziniuk and Margie Auerbach

Contents

11 You're so pretty when you're faithful to me
13 Objects of My Affection
15 Two Fuchsia Flowers
17 Bold Statements on Full-Colour Postcards or My Boyfriend Left My Love at the Gladstone Hotel
19 Breakfast on Ossington Wouldn't Be the Same Without You
20 Only One of You Will Continue
21 PTSD
22 August Through November
24 Cup Your Hands Around the Word
26 Replicate: An Amorphous Conversation
28 Bloor Street Between Clinton and Christie
30 Sobriety Is Just Something [Unlikely] We're Doing with Our Day
32 Homewreck
33 Timeless
34 Silhouette
35 How To Be Perfect Men
37 Reasons Not to Clean
38 It Must Be Stopped
39 Poem for Palestine
43 Bistro 422 or An Unclear Relationship to Danger
45 Harvest
46 A Little Rusty
48 Livingston Manor, 2008

51　You walk like a healthy meal
53　Vatican
54　Dolphin Poetry
57　Your Ghost
58　Platonic
59　Post-Partum
60　Cocktail
61　Vigil for Vasyl
65　Tread
67　Throat
69　Fibrous
71　Through the Night
73　Swallow
74　Rockabilly
75　The Perks of Being a Pretty Girl
78　No Hits
79　Toronto-Pittsburgh
80　Blood Money
81　Geography Is Inconsistent
82　Journal of Cities Parted
83　Good Good Things
84　55 Gould
85　All Tomorrow's Parties
86　Brand New Made-Up Heartbreak
87　Greenwich Mean Time (+3)
88　Taslich: Elora

89 Cargo/Vancouver
91 Cargo/Vancouver (2)
92 Collect
93 Late Payment Fee
94 We Will Not Leave Notes
95 Drunken Butterfly
96 Titles for a Book Told in Photographic Memory
97 Dark Blue Ocean
98 Trent-Severn

You're so pretty when you're faithful to me

Objects of My Affection

Your girlfriend's rib cage cracks, bone against headboard, when you fuck her in my bed. In every poem she hits her head. Her small body breaks uncontrollably under your hot hand. A broken girl cannot cry. I am left here.

A tree house. Three new vines. Expired birthday party balloons. Raw cane sugar. Remnants are just that: reminders. My hand is stamped with a stallion, the paper store, tiny icons remind me of you. Everything else small i Anna.

Your mouth on her makes you forget lyrics, the song you chose your name from. Makes you think about girls marked with black ink tattoos, thousands of miles down the coast. The song the radio played (the day you thought your life might be important) led to a crush on a deadly-wrong girl.

Your heart faltered over a dead dog.

When the song I loop tells me every little thing she does is magic, I think about older men and awards shows. We have an amicable conversation about pop songs and the girls who cover this one. It is stark, naked and maimed. It is also Anna. The girlfriend who still wears your bruises after three and a half years. You stole her youth, though you are the same age.

I want Anna's health insurance, to get me through the night. Her warm whiskey offerings. A prescription to cure me of her cold.

Tara-Michelle Ziniuk

In the corner of the dingy bar we all thought we were over, peeled, dark wood-finish railing and one step up, I step into the girl who takes my breath away. She's in from out of town, leaving soon and unthreatening. She has a dog, warm like summer and old like punk, and two friends waiting for her outside. I don't kiss girls, so know that when I open my mouth I am not doing anything that will hurt you. Her kiss skins my knee. I bandage it and come home. I don't explain and you don't ask me to. I leave gauze on your bathroom floor in protest.

We eat soft foods that night. Over-boiled and understated. No one asks for salt. When you fall asleep with the entire comforter pulled up around you, I lie beside you and do not tap or probe or bother. Had we known what would become of us in March, you wouldn't have done it. When I try to make decisions, they aren't so that you do not leave me anymore. I am not fooled by last fucks or flurries, by arms wrapped around me, never letting me go. These things do not only happen once. Would they, I would let them, remain trapped in your knowing nightclub lights, moving as I stand underneath and turn. Manual, monotone, monotonous.

This is our analogue adventure. This is you showing up after the band has finished. This is you calling from Downsview an hour after you were supposed to be here. This is me deleting the message. This is my postcard home, cursive and uncreative.

Two Fuchsia Flowers

(after Sina Queyras' "Scrabbling," from *Slip*)

You bring out Battleship as an analogy.
I make gazpacho because,
although it is springtime, it is
also almost Outremont and soup
makes sense for this. Van Horne is always within reach.

We are forever at (Stop The) war
and so this is where it gets complicated (It's Complicated).
Is (ending the) preoccupation
simply that? To love S. now is to self-loathe.
Do I have bigger fish (battles) to fry?

reading poetry makes me
write (poetry)
poetry makes me
dream think
poetry.

I am left with
two fuchsia flowers,
ink dying their water.
Ones I've imagined, but never met.

Tara-Michelle Ziniuk

Now I hold them close because
you brought them.

I want to stretch words out—take up the page with the extent that you are/have been—but all it really takes is three.

I do not have to, must not,
attribute valves to brains or
ashtrays to mechanical hearts,
as though mine is this—
evade like another,
when all
that exists
is that I am so glad for you.

Bold Statements on Full-Colour Postcards or My Boyfriend Left My Love at the Gladstone Hotel

Eyelids: puffy, translucent, yellow.
Air hits exposed skin, uncovered by
sweat, winter duvet and ripped satiny polyester.
This should be you.
My skin does not care for air.

Forget: blackberries growing in my backyard, after a day.
My cleanest joy.
We picked these and I chose you.
You made me a better poet.

My lover is jealous of the man
who serves me breakfast on Sundays,
who checks-in with me when he has not given me his full attention.

You could have taken two weeks, confessed then.
To disco ball distractions, that every tassel mattered.

I go outside and come back empty.
Exchange wild basil transplants
for this love.

Tara-Michelle Ziniuk

What I Know You Know:

From Berlin you write that there are stencils everywhere: Anne Frank in a keffiyeh.

You like colour combinations: bright turquoise and dark hot pink. I see this on the subway steps, striped with pale speckled grey, walking in front of me. Embraced on an escalator, a young man and his girlfriend: possessive, this is mine. Unable to see where they're going. The full-contact consumption you adore.

Breakfast on Ossington Wouldn't Be the Same Without You

When you get off
I think about breakfast and your face.
I like this.

When I brunch alone,
I placate, eat an excess of pork.
Learn that bacon cooks better in my bad pan,
think about weekend fixes and
How I never break glasses or eggs,
Even though both break today.

A trip to Price Chopper confirms
there are no boxes to move in.
I live above a general store in Little Portugal,
and they too say no.
I try not to be fatalistic.
Daydream, break eggs.
Small casualties,
thinking of you.

You love rye,
or is it pumpernickel?

Only One of You Will Continue

We place bets on boundaries.
Decide who will get hurt first
as fated by who becomes
America's Next Top Model.

When CariDee wins
I open the door,
Expecting you to be there.

PTSD

My therapist laughs
every time she says:
"Post-Traumatic Stress Disorder."

If I were to hear PTSD
Without the subsequent laughter
I might be triggered.

August Through November

You say, "I always go for the pretty girls" and then you go.

My knees fail to buckle and my heart fails to skip. I've tried this melodrama before, and even it is failing me. You shoot me the saddest stare as some sort of evidence, proof that you hurt, too. I try slamming the door, but the hinges won't let me. Our ending is anticlimactic and muted.

I am usually solutions-based— all answers and fix-its. This time I am tired.

Picking a clay coffee mug out from dirty dishwater, I throw it against the cheap wallpapered wall; burnt sienna smashes against the glossy cherry print. It hardly makes a sound. The dark insides of the clay stare up at me, shards across linoleum, all wants. I'd call my therapist, but she'd tell me that not everything is symbolic and to clean up the mess. Some people have husbands for this. I have her.

Summer comes and you post a photo of you and yours. You wear bright orange cotton as though it is the only option. The woman you pose with, not the colour you wear, puts a wrench in my plans.

I pack everything I can into Tupperware the night you post that photo. My life is compartmentalized into oddly sized rectangles and small microwave-melted cylinders— instant temporary vessels that proclaim I'm not really going anywhere. Even leaving doesn't mean anything. I ask you to carry my bags and you do.

My memory is as roundabout as we are. I announce our endings, but never our beginnings. Rattle off details and possible last straws in haphazard lists on sheets pulled from a Country Kittens notepad. We are all threats. We are one lyric off. We are fine, and from August through November, fine is finally perfect.

In the afternoons, when I smell of men's cologne and magazine pages, I wonder what the others have found that we have not.

Between Saturn's return and down payments, I know that this is not weak, wrong or original. This does not pain me, does not trip me up, does not make me nervous.

Three times a year, from the ages of 26 to 28, I want a baby in 8-day spurts. I hold my shoulders back on subway platforms, thorax intact, and middle bursting to be acknowledged. I wonder if everyone riding southbound to Union Station knows. This becomes one more future we do not discuss.

Cup Your Hands Around the Word

> "Cup your hands around the word:
> August . . . It's as bitter as beer and
> trembles in delicious agony like sleep
> and apples and suspended breath."
> —Chandra Mayor, *August Witch*

It may not be August yet, but all my letters are here. They are bitter with distaste and celebratory like medicine and Seder plate herbs. Nothing can stop us now, nothing.

On Grey's Anatomy they say everything twice. Twice, they say everything. The scripting is comfortably predictable like wanting them to fall back in love, and back in love. Back, in love. They relocate commas like everything changes.

Like I do
   with space.

We cannot format the truth. Could have never predicted this, even though we did.
Even though Metro Morning told us not to.
All this is costing us is our freelance jobs.

You, send me an email telling me you're moving because you cannot afford to come to my birthday dinner— that you've packed your bags, and are leaving.
(I heard you the first time.)

I don't even ask when it was you unpacked. I don't even ask for my keys. I don't even ask you to do your fucking dishes. (I don't even try.)
I scripted this three weeks ago. I scripted this in April. I scripted this in October. I threw out the first round of lines because I knew I'd see them again, and then again. And that's why, Alex, and that's why I can't take you back.

I reply in nice enough lines, out-of-character exclamation points and jokes I'd never make if I were acting more like myself,
but ever since this became a medical drama, it's all been so much easier. It's all been, coasting. It's all been, blonde girls with bleached teeth on clinic floors named after dead ex-boyfriends, with 48 hour on-call shifts and perfect roller curls in-tact. You go, girl. I hope you find that baby you put up for adoption. I hope you find, your baby.

Replicate: An Amorphous Conversation

We talk about replication and not doing that but I know
that if I don't eat I can feel everyone who's touched me in my stomach (red curry
and all that was hers), and all I want are hands, mouths, faces like birds and fish
flitting.

We talk about replication and I tape every face I've seen to worn locker walls,
vaulted between dry ribs, threatening to let out breath.
I spoon grainy natural peanut butter mortar into the cracks of this, sew myself
back together with pens designed for injection— somebody else's condition.

I take any break I can and break everything in sight,
see only coveted porcelain plates, blue glass shards of where a house used to
be, a decorative plaque meaning something unreadable.

These are the things we speak of when we do not speak of divorce:
-plans
-paper
-planes
-sides of highways and bruises that will last longer than this. Bruises that may
outlive either of us. Angry, angry sex because we both know this is true.

On the insides of the strips of Scotch tape there are tiny photos of us. The photos
are ants— tiny inkblot tests to see if you are paying attention. You tell me you
remember these photos being taken. I go home. When I get home a note is

already there, written on a cue card: I know those are ants. It takes so little to relieve me that I am scared. Scared that you can pretend not to pay attention to the point, that every time you take note I will take it as a compliment.

We talk about replication as mice take over my brand new apartment. I wait for my landlord as though he is coming, like Elijah or a second chance. Like waiting to get over macrocosms and over-investments. I sit on the couch perfectly still hoping for someone to find me. Like this will help. Like the instructions said, Stay Perfectly Still. I pretend mice have never reigned before.

Bloor Street Between Clinton and Christie

In line with my penchant for
bad decisions and
melancholy narratives,
I leave a warm house with warm company
to drink at the local tavern alone.

I find fashion in passersby
and love in celebrity crushes (we never mention *him*, Marshall Mathers).
They would find me neither
stylish nor lovely.
Wonder if I do/would want that,
do not consider myself one to want.

Upon entering Korea Town
there's a luminescent tiger
large bowls of chicken ginseng soup,
the corner where Kingston, my former roommate, was jumped
and the shop where Jana bought walnut cakes for the radio station's overnight
fundraising drive.

At the sunken park where the cops encircled us,
batons against plastic shields,
flashback screams,
I can hardly remember my name.

Premature

1.

I do not wake up from this. 1981
My mother in a red, cable-knit sweater,
flurry of snowfall, ice on the ground,
she steps out of a cab.
My mother was not rushed to the hospital,
or if so, not to Emergency
(At least not in the month I was born)
maybe bleeding, five months prior.
This snowstorm, for certain, did not happen on May 27th
—would have been a better story if it had.

Long, dark hair, 114 pounds at the end of her term,
pre-packed suitcase in hand,
she is brought stuffed bears instead
of Camel Lights and
palms stuffed with sweaty heroin in tin.

2.
At the gentrifier lesbian bar,
they track conception dates:
November, nine months after Valentine's Day,
September, nine post New Year's Eve.
One woman dates her conception as "after an Alice Cooper show" and
marks herself unwanted.
I count eight months from my conception, a different kind of split-screen showing
want and un-want.

Tara-Michelle Ziniuk

Sobriety Is Just Something [Unlikely] We're Doing with Our Day

On television, I watch a wide-toothed boy kick a girl after debate club to signify that he likes her. I tell you about it the next night. And I tell you that I hate you, an expression of my resurfacing adolescence, this truly uncomfortable crush.

This is obvious, but I start to look at your mouth instead of your eyes, where your shoulder meets your chest, instead of your hand-printed buttons or the emblem on your shirt.

I step into and against you, stop and expect.
Do not ask if I can spend the night, or if you are spending, . . .
Just stay, or do not.
I don't know where I learned this (I'd like to pretend).

It is fundamental that I don't like anything about you. This is why we're friends. When I want to kiss you, I think that we will never speak again.

The fact that I can imagine exactly where every part of you hurts me when you collapse drunk from above me makes me (not only) angry.

When you ask why we never do this sober, I reply:
"Sober— your girlfriend.
Sober— because we're pretending not to do this at all.
Sober— I know that song."

Even when I liked it at age fourteen, at summer camp academy for the socially demented genius, I never would have dated you.

It is this inane dementia that has me imagining myself locking my fingers in your hair.

I have never wanted sexual tension so much as wanting to be:
A muse
A relief
A breaker (of rules or ground)
Pretty.

Pretty doesn't have to be the smartest girl you've ever known, even if she is. Doesn't have to follow you to the bar, into the arms of dance-floor barroom girls, or home. Pretty doesn't have to pretend you don't have a girlfriend.

Wanting you is like wanting a bullet, in a state where suicide is illegal.

Homewreck

Synonym for "affair"
Less than ten syllables
Twenty-three Scrabble points

Timeless

So often,
time gets measured in relationships.

Time stopped
When I started not-really seeing you.

Silhouette

Two figures pass in a dark alley.
You forget me as soon as I am gone.
Your girlfriend screams as her head hurts against the brick wall.
She does not forget me.

You draw figure eights sideways, like infinity signs, with your index finger on the tabletop next to your napkin. You pretend to quit smoking.

I slide individual bean sprouts out of my spring roll. My fingers burn and jump— a rhythm not unlike my jerking you off. I do not mention that this crosses my mind. I do not mention the E. coli bacteria.

You
give
girls
eating
disorders.

I miss you when you're not here.S

How To Be Perfect Men

1.

Post 9-11, Women In Black hold signs above my menorah: "Our Grief Is Not A Cry For War"

2.

Every sad mix CD has a song about a basement on it. We do a keyword search for "waiting" and when I finally remember you, every song I hear makes me feel like I'm on hold. You record me calling you a jerk, over and over. It is playful, but I am still embarrassed when I listen to this mix for the first time in a car full of people I barely know. You could not have hoped for more.

3.

I watch men on television build what television tells us is Israel's first planned city. Vodka volcanoes in my diet 7-up as they stew tomatoes over fire and ask each other about the relative attractiveness of the women who patrol the checkpoints that eject them: "How tall?" and "Does she have a small mouth?" Wishing the translations were more coherent, I wonder about the Arabic letter for the hard "c" sound, if there is one. I picture my father in a manger and realize it might not have been Jerusalem, but there's no way of knowing 1950.

Leftovers From My Cancelled Party

Peacock headdress
Velvet coat with hand cream in pocket
Bright pink tunnel (Slurpee straw)
Songs To Die To
Ken doll-coloured penis straw, undoubtedly from the Condom Shack, salvaged from Yael's bachelorette party
Large piece of vegan chocolate cake, many forks
Raspberry pie with my initials baked in, fresh raspberries, cornstarch
One lotus leaf from sticky rice
One stack of never-seen-before striped shirts and unworn underwear
A hole in my heart the size of a tube of MAC Ruby Woo A55
A photo of a boy and a beer I slept with once
Ninety-six percent of my body hair in the bathtub, Neet in the laundry basket
Two wooden shoes
A fear of my heaviest metal friend
A sadness toward the friends I like most
A bit of confusion
A birthday vow to stop getting in cars with drunk drivers
Glass in my foot from dancing on Christmas lights in the kitchen
Wildflower seeds from a wedding
My door frame, in the hallway. When did that happen?
The plastic shot glass by the bathtub I thought I could dip my fingers in, to drip cold water on your neck
A metal travel mug of three-day-old water I thought you could drink from, as though you were going somewhere.
Then again (poetically, passive-aggressively), you always were.

Reasons Not to Clean

The armchair is a tangle of ribbon,
strings of pearls and cream-coloured sequins,
white on white
on dirty plush pale.

It Must Be Stopped

My mother calls every year on World AIDS Day
because I am "into that."

She calls every year on Pride
and asks, "Isn't it World AIDS Day today, or something?"

One Chanukah she commits a cardinal gift-buying sin,
and gets me Clothes with Words on Them.

The clothes are pyjamas, printed 100 times all over the long pants and sleeves:
"Housework is Evil, It Must Be Stopped."

"Mom!"

"What! It's like a protest. You *like* protests."

Ladies and gentlemen: my mother.

Poem for Palestine

"The missiles can go where we cannot. But how can you send love with a missile?"
—Ussama Abu el-Sheikh, 19, Shatila refugee camp, Beirut, August 2006

I didn't buy the Dead Sea soap imported from Israel,
or the olive oil for Palestinian rights either.
I couldn't afford them.

I smashed a mug with Rachel Corrie's face on it today.
Not because it was meaningless to me
but because today, if my grandparents had one slightly progressive friend—
not to worry, because they don't—
Lebanon would look like a photo of Rachel Corrie's face.

When, at the beginning of a road trip, enclosed in the back of the car,
someone asks what I think of the union boycott on Israeli goods,
I mutter something about being "into it."
"But what right do they have?" she demands,
"It's not like they're Middle Eastern scholars."
But that's all she can come up with.

When he called Montreal
to report being detained in the occupied territory,
I wanted to ask who sent him,
if we'd raised all of that money

Tara-Michelle Ziniuk

because we didn't believe that people who lived there
were already filling those cells,
fighting in those cells.
I wanted to tell him we were occupying an office,
that it was late, Eastern Standard Time.

We took shifts in the office,
left only for phone cards or extension cords or address books,
called his mother and lawyer back home.

When he returned, he told us that in the camps,
they didn't know about the demos,
the pressure we were putting on government,
media campaigns.
He said they knew only of the boycotts,
urged us to continue.

And when he stood up in front of the room to report unrecognized villages,
demolition orders, F-16s overhead,
White phosphorous melting skin and bones, burned bridges.
When he told us the population is unemployed,
and a cab ride costs a thousand Canadian dollars,
OCAP denounced the demolition of a basketball court.

It will never matter how much I care about the children of Etobicoke.
That will never have been a war crime,
not *Working From The Inside*,
not *Personal Is Political* or *Struggle Starts At Home*.

I stopped playing the game where I show people my Hebrew tattoos,
say "Well my dad was Israeli" to justify my stance on "Talmudic genocide"
or divisions between Jews.
With that,
I will never be enough.

In the backseat of this unpaid-for SUV, you are just Israeli enough,
you are just Jewish enough to count.
One vote against the boycott,
One vote is sometimes all that matters.

I have no votes to give to cut power supplies to hospitals,
to a quarter of a country's population internally displaced,
to twenty-eight years in prison without trial, to forty percent of cluster bombs still planted.
Call me anti-Semitic— my blood family does.

When, during a Q&A session, in the middle of a crowd,
someone asks who is the, *uh*, Nelson Mandela of this fight,
I want to tell him
that it's not OCAP,
not the guy we sent to that cell so many miles away,
not the U.S. war photographer who sent snapshots home.
That at this rate, we may never know.

Bistro 422 or An Unclear Relationship to Danger

1.

The day you take down the photos of her
I take some down too, also her.
The day you become mine,
you also become the world's.

Pre-emptively, I said
the safest way to have you,
was to have you belong to her.

Now I sidetrack at misplaced stares,
hasty references,
and what they all want— you.

2.

I repeat strings of salty words
you told me: you drank enough to kiss her
eight months into picturing it
and she told you it was too late,
wrapped you around her slender wrist,
burned into you the words *Not Right Now*.

Tara-Michelle Ziniuk

The sentence you spoke when you told me,
or the back patio, that plastic wasteland,
that you got your girlfriend off on the bench I sat on.
I shifted to the left, sure that all infection was hers
(though I liked her and was indifferent to disease),
and could not possibly belong to punk bar barf
or six-dollar liquor pitchers in any other form.
I slid backward in my seat, pulled the short straw out of the deep liquid.

Harvest

Track my annual income by the going weight of squash:
Acorn, Pepper, Butternut or Spaghetti.
How many times per hour
can I make him come
at the rate of $4.39/kg?

A Little Rusty

"I feel like a robot but my eyes are crying," you say
in the numb spot of a break-up.
This time you did the breaking,
and what you broke was me.
Only your eyes were sad.

In the morning I ask how you feel.
"A little rusty," is your reply.
I draw a boy with a box for a head,
cut holes for eyes.
Beneath his snowflake sweater, ripe with asterisks, I scrawl
A little rusty.
It's the least I could do, and more than I should have.

When the last straw turns out to be glass,
I am here, splintered and stupid.
You leave town like anyone would.
I paint my face with the day,
make it match this already red town.
Like my mouth it is never really yours.
This ugly, marker-bleed town
makes me write in black ink, but even black clashes here.

On the wall of your work,
when no one was looking,
Someone wrote ROBOT
in red letters, like curls, but
they don't make you think of me.
You see only the spite, not the swirly lines.

You call me to ask about coincidence— scolding tone.
I tell you the word is "karma," not coincidence.
You don't believe any of it, so I write it in red.
But even that's been done, and done to death.
My green eyes can't watch this anymore.

Tara-Michelle Ziniuk

Livingston Manor, 2008

A convenient technical error erases me from a photo:
Smiling tired faces lined up in front of a covered bridge.

In town (Liberty, NY), the man running the beautiful vintage shop confides
that his partner, who died last winter,
left all these precious things that he knows very little about.

Over Boggle, we're still fine.
The striped sweater, the faulty car, the couple with the meeting to get back to,
Will not know of Sunday, will hear of it only in grapevine recaps and later
absences that no one will discuss.

A yellow pinwheel turns to the sky.
The sky opens, lends lead and steel rain.

Archipelago plays the whole way home.

Me in a green ribbed tank top, grey cut-off sweats.
Me as a nightshade.
Me as 6 a.m. dew. (I didn't see it coming, I turned my head.)

You walk like a healthy meal

Vatican

I decide my occupational fate
when you tell me that they keep
the Popes' hearts lined up in jars
in basement corridors of the Vatican.
There are no more obstacles here than any other job prospect.

And I do like found hearts,
shaped from leaves and especially of metal.
Obscured only slightly by living in the Anglo art student area of Montreal,
scattered with intentional hearts.

I picture them pulsing
like the kidneys and malfunctioned foetuses in the Mutter Museum:
Formaldehyde and dark poultry blood through worryingly thin skin.

I imagine you or some knight,
finding me there in 3017,
like something engraved into a lamppost outside an apartment in the Mile End,
thinking they'd live there forever,
not imagining you or this or now.

Tara-Michelle Ziniuk

Dolphin Poetry

I had a can of soup
and I would have given that to you.
I had a heart— hard like a horse's,
a pony on a locket,
weak teeth,
nothing you would have wanted.

I would have given everything for you.
It sounds bigger than anything.
I never had a country to give:
I had a shitty apartment,
less shitty than many peoples' apartments,
and I would have given you the bed.
(Even though I swore after my birthday, when everyone but you took the bed
and nobody but you apologized,
that I'd never give up the bed again.)

I had a silver shoe,
a stained glass goldfish,
a tube of glycerin.

Sequins, beads and gloss that looked good to men on the street.

I had a dictionary of words I couldn't make you take.
Like leftovers: left and over.

I put my arms up to the sky, but it was never as big as you,
could not stretch or shake or believe our truth.
There was a long list like:
    Dinosaurs
    Unicorns
    Dragons
    Seahorses
    Stallions
    Loch Ness
I would have given them all to you
but I had none. None, and a wave crashing.

I would have given my right left hands for you—
    the sides of my brain

I would have used all these words I'm too shallow to utter.

I would have become a children's wading pool, a weigh station or a roadmap for you.

An atlas. A glass of water. A stethoscope.
If any of it would have helped.

Tara-Michelle Ziniuk

I would have been
the last cup of coffee
in my mother's house
and not asked
you to split it 2 ways.

I would have only ever said the right thing
and had it mean what I wanted it to.

I wouldn't have needed it.
Or I wouldn't have needed it all.
Or I wouldn't have needed it all to end neatly.

Your Ghost

You do not return phone calls. I stay up all night, waiting for the knock, or phone to ring, afraid to be startled, but determined not to be.

Each time I turn the corner to my apartment door, I picture tripping over your knee. I picture you sitting on the landing, legs crossed. My breath changes. You are an image I hold onto because, that once, you startled me.

Nights of summer cider sensor lights and the impulse to open the door to the backyard. The ashtray girl might have been there. (Sometimes she left treasures in threes, lined up my street. Small blue screwdrivers, stencils on cement.)

At this point, I expect, you'd just call, with "Hey, how's it going?" like nothing, invisible.

Missing people is the most impersonal thing.

Tara-Michelle Ziniuk

Platonic

This winter,
everything tastes gourmet
or else like it was prepared by Food Not Bombs.
It doesn't really matter.

Yael says you know you're actually hungry if the answer is lentils.
I get the joke/am sentimental, but
it all tastes the same today.

Yellow zucchini in chicken stock,
fresh from the year-round farmers' market,
stew of wilting collards,
waxy boxed chocolate.
It all tastes like winter and wanting.

Your matted hair beside me,
rewinding the tape we never manage to watch all the way through,
swallowing sticky thirds of pills.
Thick, unsweetened cranberry juice
half-and-half for coffee, all-night convenience and other things
we manage to never take for granted.

Post-Partum

Call it separation anxiety
when I replace you with the Internet.
I am G's iPod—
What she got when she couldn't get the girl,
what she broke when my heart was too hard.
You only wish I could replace you.

Cocktail

My brain is where my heart should be.
I think too much.
Fortunately for me,
my heart doubles as a Molotov cocktail.

Vigil for Vasyl

South Parkdale: King and Jameson
four cop cars, six visible cops, arresting two people,
a couple, or maybe she is his mother.
I check to see how tight the cuffs are;
too small to scream, too clean to notice,
not used to either of these things.

Angry at the activists down the street
for not being here,
still I drift toward them.

There are memories around every bend,
at 1510 as well.
I picture this place so often,
I forget what it actually looks like.

It feels typical
to walk up to the crowd encircled by police,
on my own.

Just scruffy enough that the cops don't call me Ma'am.
They do ask if I am trying to get by,
would like to go around.

Tara-Michelle Ziniuk

Here: 3 cop cars,
1 van,
1 paddy wagon. Oh,
and bikes.

On the wall, projections of our protest,
long ago at this same site.
When the crowd shots become huddles of people in coats,
I turn away. I'd left by the time the temperature dropped.

The guy who jeopardized things during the action
does not pass the torch when it circles.
Eventually the flame goes out.
No one acts surprised.
No one is.
Someone puts a tea light
on a two-foot concrete wall to compensate,
but the wind will have none of it.

They play Johnny Cash,
of whom the deceased, apparently, was always a fan.
The moment of silence is two men
talking loudly about Cash's politics.
The song is the Nine Inch Nails cover,

tackier still on the occasion of a suicide.
The crowd goes wild with self-righteous ignorance.

During the muted, tearful speeches,
I picture myself summers ago—
whiskey, ripped denim skirt and the man who was on my mind.
And the rest:
the backyard of the building,
the neighbour over the fence,
the corduroy couches on the balcony,
the light fixtures inside.
I have cried here before,
though never next to a black and white photo of a man,
blown up large like a Pepsi ad (though he holds a can of Coke).

The girl behind me just moved here from B.C.
Other people's lives lost
are always, somehow, so close to home.
We are three city blocks from my apartment;
two from where I lived then.
This is not my ended life.

I ask the only friend I have there to walk my way.
Between Maynard and Brock
we discuss other appropriated deaths, mostly homeless.
The decision, time and time again
to position members' meetings
as more important than anything else
(the wounded, dead, discarded, irrelevant).
Someone else can always respond, and will.

There was a time before they all had social service jobs,
when the homeless people finally got fed up
with the activists who got them all arrested
and ultimately left them to resist on the inside, alone.

I thought that would be the end, of this,
a fabricated existence.

Yet, moments ago,
I thought: It would be easy to go back.
And it would be.

Tread

I am walking
and for once, this town is bigger than you.

I am walking and thinking
about what it means to be the only one you've left,
if that's even true.

I am walking and churning up earth
feeling the plastic embedded in the backs of my shoes crack.

I am walking and realizing
my feet might be flatter
or my spine might be bent
or my hip rotated forward.

I am walking and forget that Guelph is not America.
Imagine if I took the job there,
we could stay up until eleven and think it was late,
talk about how non-violent direct action doesn't work,
and how kids have to learn for themselves,
drinking white wine that neither of us knows the name of.

Febreze smells like teenagers smoking to me,
like affairs, like mice scratching the insides of old drywall.

Febreze is a fraud and it makes me think of Amber in Paris.

I am walking and daydreaming
about owning a home and rows of lettuce.
How, I never would have believed if you told me
that today I'd have my natural hair colour
or that I'd ever dream of lettuce.

I am walking and the city is walking on my back,
crunching it like a number.

Throat

She likes getting fucked when she can't breathe
but I can never breathe
so it's not the same.

A personal ad requests strangulation by sock
and I only have mismatched socks.
So, I close my hand around her small neck,
bird rough and soft like feathers,
hard skeletal lines that tell me to stop and
my hand is too small for this too.

We never talk about this, or the personal ad.
Unlike my usual self, and contrary to what I believe in,
I say, "you like it,"
and she nods,
and she does.

I don't think about my own lungs
or the blue ones tattooed to his middle finger
until a postcard with an image of a ball-gag arrives,
tucked into a white envelope inside a box of books.
Faint pencil-crayon text tells me I am not pretty, but someone was.
This is what it takes to take my breath away,
illness and asthma and panic attacks aside.

I throw everything plastic out of my house that day:
margarine containers and dog toys,
soap dishes and spray bottles.
Press on my own padded ribcage,
wonder what it would take to get in.

Fibrous

Everything is imperfect today.
The prescription I can't afford to fill hurts,
fibrous paintbrush stems coat the insides of my eyelids.

Pinwheel on the fridge, a list out of 20.
What Not To Eat
Everything's a risk, and yet
I like fermented foods— soy, dairy, syrup, fruit sugar—
all more than latex, sea salt water, raw cashews.
Amoxicillin, Benzodiazepine, Pseudoephedrine
Goldenseal and so on.
Avocados and my mattress have never seemed so irritating.

No wheel tells hormones where not to go.
No book with a checklist to defy anatomy:
Hope and Help For.

The nurse at the anonymous clinic asks if I know what this is about.
"Wheat," I want to tell her, a modern, believable lie—like yoga or pomegranate or probiotics.

Instead, I pull up my sleeve,
put out the inside of my arm and allow her to draw blood.

December 6 (Dufferin Station)

Leaving the up/down bound platform to
wind tunnel heating vents and chips clipped to a stand.
Must be unclear-charity-pizza day, dollar-a-slice, because
all I can hear is change in metal jars
buckets of bills and "Dollar, a dollar!"

This time it's commemorative.
Persuasive thirty-eight-year-old men bellow
"In 1989! ...
It's for a good cause."
("I know about the cause.")
Is this your way of picking up women,
or doing your daughter a favour?

Unsure if I'm supposed to feel guilty
for not contributing my bus money
or for being alive.

"Massacre, massacre,"
yelled into the hyperventilated synthetic air system
like buckets of beer for sale at a sports game.

Through the Night

> *"I'm for anything that gets you through the night, be it prayer, tranquilizers or a bottle of Jack Daniels."*
> —Frank Sinatra, 1968 interview with *Playboy*

There is no seduction, only suggestion.
I taunt with words against the academy and can't help but think,
He wants that Oscar, when I say
the Academy.
And, Thank you.

On the porch I repeat over and over:
"I am course material
but have never attended a course."
Of course.

I'm for anything
that gets you through the night.
A warm body
hot water bottle
Degrassi special features.
I'm all for take-out in bed,
crumbs, spilled shake from the bottom of the bag,
and lipstick on pillowcases.
Knowing where sweat combines
is scientific proof that it's all about pheromones.

Is he hot for her, on my sheets, or me?
Everyone wants all-day breakfast,
but no one wants to wash the bedding.
It's getting old, the analogy.
We're all getting old.
Maybe this is what lube is for.
Or maybe it's for people who never liked each other anyway.

We wake up to your mom calling.
She thinks it's a good idea for you to stagehand on the set of
Menopause Out Loud.
I ask if she's having a mid-life crisis,
if maybe your girlfriend is
uncomfortable; think about church cheese and pre-packaged single ham slices,
peanut noodles, and the math. 69 cents + a dollar a bag, bring a canned good for me and
whether she'd be all

"Meat is Murder," if she wasn't poor.
And what a rich girl could do for her
you, your mom, mine, any of it.
I'm so hard for. Hard up for. Spare a dollar or hold my beer while I.

There is no seduction, only suggestion.
Let me walk you home.

Swallow

Even the swallows
tattooed to her chest
are upset.

They are not credible
or original.
It is hard
to compliment a symbol
that tries so hard.

Rockabilly

You're wearing a liar's heart
taped to your sleeve
like a rockabilly tattoo.
No dice.

The Perks of Being a Pretty Girl

People only spin the bottle
when there's someone in the room they want to kiss.

Cold air blows through the vent.
Takes money to make money
and this comes before heat.

I have to pee when I get to work, but
I'm late. Instead,
I'm swung in circles,
legs around a new man's waist.
Who could predict this as a fetish?

My brother says "I'm around for anything,"
to indicate that he won't show.
Bet you didn't know I had a brother.

I update my website to make myself feel famous,
search songs I've never heard
just to quote them online.

Find a new boyfriend on the Internet,
in the background of a photo.
I click through 256 friends to find him,
sure that this is finally love.

Tara-Michelle Ziniuk

Picking a boyfriend based on a crowd shot
is *totally* like dating the drummer.

The worst thing for a poet
is being told to go write a poem about it.
This week I am told to write a poem about:
rooftops in Brooklyn, failed friendships and the mice that would not die.

She asks "How are you?"
the question that makes me cry.

I buy green grapes,
even though they remind me of my mother
and say, "She should have died, not him."
I say simple things that are heavy and regular in movies.
My mother says "People were saying that at the funeral."

I dream my grandmother dead
to have something in common with someone.
I overestimate myself.

Listen to recently borrowed CDs,
and deem them nostalgia,
having borrowed them before.

My archivist tendencies
are lost to faith in the Internet
My sentimentality now lives
in a folder marked for deletion after 30 days.
Panic-framed pressure I never succumb to.

Fern finds Madison's new partner between her legs.
Looking through them on a yoga mat
in a classroom the fire department would throw fits over,
she knows why they're together.

A smashed car is being taken to surgery,
loaded on another vehicle.
I say "Ow" as it passes,
imagine the car saying it back to me,
then image search guts until they're pretty.

Move wires with tools for you.
Don't pay my bills, am cut off.
But, like a good drunk, refuse to accept this.

Using the flat-edge pulled out from the nail clippers,
I untwist exposed wire from the cord.
No new messages.
The Rogers guy seems baffled by my disappointment.

No Hits

You will never find what you're looking for in me.

Toronto-Pittsburgh

At a dreary eight in the morning,
on board a darkened commuter train,
I kiss an 18-year-old kid who's escaped
from his post in the Israeli Defense Force.

Because I am a slut, or an asshole,
or because I never knew my father.
Or maybe because I am just trying to connect
with the homeland.

Blood Money

History:
These bills are covered in blood,
digits pulled from orifices,
Type-O ties parted.

Pulled from mid-1940s Poland
B'nai Brith summer camp soup pots
insulin and heroin fixes, black velvet paintings
sketches on insides of cigarette packs,
thirty-year-old perfume,
dusty sheer scarves stuffed in purses, five-part candelabra,
my grandfather's empty side of the bed,
fuzzy plastic fruit,
laminated placemats,
water-damaged basement apartments.

These bills are bled with adult supervision,
basketball hoops without nets,
black-eyed peas burning fire departments to our block,
cop shop up the street,
locks on bedroom doors (on the inside this time),
full threats,
mismatched linoleum posing as tile,
estranged boyfriends in backward baseball caps,

knock-off Danier leather,
cheaper-yet mimics of Lancôme's Trésor,
brothers in gaudy and cracked photo frames.

Geography Is Inconsistent
Geography is Not Timeless, Predictable or Consistent.

1.

Union Station
Jealous: the girl with the MacBook, Starbucks tall mild.
Behind the tracks, a man-made lake.
A text message confronts me with: "a lumpy throat, like I've ruined everything."
And I will love you forever.

2.

At the bookstore on Ossington,
my mother makes immense declarations,
hollow, booming and soiled.
I disclaim to the man
and his constant companion, the Revlon blue-black girl.
Buy four books with guilt, not money,
when she goes outside to smoke.

3.

Barcelona
Tags that I will never know.
You dream of an ex,
stumble drunk against a friend's lips.
What mine are:
Cobblestone, aged and unreliable.

Journal of Cities Parted

Nothing was ever meant to be hidden,
that's not what we were doing.
Your bedroom walls, Galleria Anna, did not speak well of you,
though they spoke honestly.

Picture the car you drove in:
I never quite can.
Picture pelicans instead,
both of us.
Scan the lining of the roof interior
formed with finger oils
for any kind of clue—
a condom wrapper or cassette case.

The long-distance ring, mine this time, and the green and white socks must give you away.

It is like fucking Anna has become summer
and I, an 8-hour bus ride.

Good Good Things

1.

On a scrap of paper, you write:
"Love songs on Pandora make me think of you."
Finally the Internet is good for something.

The paper gets lost between declarations of love; forever, promise and pinkie swear. Words you write to the sweet-faced, exemplary skin, eyes down the perfect bridge of her nose
girl, who adores you unconditionally, who will continue to despite your shoddy future plans and present-tense pretenses.

2.

It is a Monday night when, in rare form, my mouth knows what's important to me. I wake up gagging on a faltering throat (my own), run to the bathroom with a mouth full of blood. And spit.

3.

Girls in barrettes and angel wing pendants sing bluesy folk covers of
slowed down *Y Control*, soft stark Cat Power, Britney-made-sad. Made-sad covers are my favourite. Yours too.
The lady at Sushi D remembers your face.

In an armchair two or so city blocks from home, between Alice's house, your parents' and mine, I turn off Bon Jovi at, *It's all the same, Only the names have changed*, because he is an asshole and a liar.

55 Gould

1.

The air outside my work smells like plum sauce and cigar.
I push broken cloves into a tangerine,
Find and Replace stench with spicy fragrant fruit.

2.

My co-worker has never been as animated,
as the moment I lend him a pen.
His one word emails evolve from O.K.
to Okay.

3.

In the empty meeting room
I squeak permanent marker across a bright white dry-erase board,
feign Excel formatting for:
I always liked
when you left
in the morning.

All Tomorrow's Parties

Excited in URLs and H&M plaid,
you turn to writing in awful exclamations
that announce, you are
Just getting back!,
or On [your] way!
I quick hit reply,
wanting only to circle in red and request revisions.

You down whiskey shots
like parks are going out of season,
while I curl tea leaves at the bottom of my cup,
stir Baileys into a bodum,
clutch cracked ceramic from an office long gone.
Why else would I own a smiley face?

I stop being able to see
after the eleventh exclamation point!
Awed that so-and-so showed her tits at the bar!!
And knowing, life-lesson at twenty-four with keys to your parents' house, that
One Last After-Party is All That Matters.

Tara-Michelle Ziniuk

Brand New Made-Up Heartbreak

In bed my boyfriend wraps his long body around a girl whose waist is smaller than the top of my thigh,

I think about hair being removed with dense hot wax,
green and potent.
Can't turn on the stove for days.

My best friend hoes me out to boys three states away who ask if
"I'm into making out,"
which sounds to me like, "Does she fuck?"

Like it's that easy.
I've forgotten that it is.

My best friend is so lonely she kisses three girls this week.

Greenwich Mean Time (+3)

She says smart things often,
even if I don't remember what kind of bread she likes.

I stand at FedEx watching her,
under a line of clocks that show me
international time.

I spend the day distracted,
wondering what time it is in Russia.

Taslich: Elora

I tell her the gorge is like white water rafting for dummies and I'm glad to be walking along it. I'm unable to finance an inner tube rental, in any case.

Imagine a blue-eyed boy before me.
Imagine myself without longing, but this does not last for long.

We are all dissolved.

We are water on paper.

We are Yom Kippur felt-tip rising to the surface of the water off the old port.

We are tiny pieces of paper, torn breadcrumbs, regrets into the stream unless it is windy.

Our confessions tangle, crumpled from our pockets into the air; I take note not to find meaning in this.

Mary tells me the boy walking by often propositions her.

He's fifteen years her junior.

I try not to make out his face, picture them, caught in prayer and thrown on immediacy.

Erase the 'o' in the name of our Lord, replace it with a hyphen.

In the moment of a blessing, I try not to consider that either.

Cargo/Vancouver

My heart boards a bus to Vancouver.
I pass a bag of snacks from Strictly Bulk.
It's not all healthy, but it's better than what you'll find out there, Baby.
You laugh at this and the tiny glass jar of strained organic apples, marketed as baby food. *Baby*.

Popular pop-punk songs and the last people each of us dated have ruined this word for us, but I will always be yours.

Shards of me, confetti to the ground, when you open your backpack, leave something heavy behind, pretend
that you are coming back.
That this is another trip taken and, I'll see you soon, *baby*.
It's all I can do to keep my lungs in. It's all I can do to keep my hiccups from screaming, my phone from dialling itself drunk, voicemail declarations and expensive impromptu airline tickets.

I was still in high-school when I last waited for, "*I want to take you with me*"—
But I can't, wait this time.
I've been waiting for you for so long and,
love doesn't learn.
Love doesn't even take its own advice. Love is preaching to the converted. Love skipped me when handing out sermons,
or prayer books to pick up.

Love passed around a hat and I left nothing.

TV Guide has got to be joking when they call Brenda Walsh a bitch. I count in 11s and multiples of 3. Alphabetize the notes on my hand. I pour honey on the floor and research what cleans it. I stain. I stain and swallow. I smell mould and think it is you. I taste ash and think it is you (I've known it so long). I measure sugar cupped in my hand. I slouch dry into the garden and give up. I slice the outline of my hands with sharp tops of cans, mark them dead for pick up. I scratch expiry dates off and throw up residue, bleak birch bark bile. I puke into a blue bandana the day after you leave.

I send single line emails asking if you're there yet.

Cargo/Vancouver (2)

Between the green walls of the apartment where you used to love
anything enough to chase it and
me enough to return,
I tell you it hurts.
You tell me to pay to have it removed.

You add me to a list of things you cannot afford.
Stories caked under corners of fingernails you pick in a Scarborough food court, over lunch with your mother.
I wonder how I read when I show up to meet mine, when work doesn't provide a shower and she's so fond of my scandalous outfits.

Between a man-made lake and
a beautiful freight train engine under glass, you say:
"This time I'm there for you."
The things we like best are showcased, a reminder that we are not the only ones fetishizing calloused palms or industrial landscapes.
We've known this for ages but when you tell me
that you would have left her for me, that she thought that you had,
It's already too late.

A black line drawing of the CN Tower cityscape fades,
a BC mountain skyline
takes its place
and mine.

Tara-Michelle Ziniuk

Collect

A bad sign:
I take my cordless to the edge of the bathtub,
harm reduction in case you call.
In case today, unlike any other day, you need to talk,
or want to hear me, or she's out, or I'm worth
the time it takes to call collect.

A bad sign:
When I am waiting
for something awful enough
that I can justify the phone ringing at her house.

Late Payment Fee

When I check mail on Thursday,
It's all bills.

Unfortunately for romance,
Airmail almost always contains bad news.

We Will Not Leave Notes

1.

This is me with Anna's hands.
Watch a photo form in front of us,
what I look like when you can't see me:
your ex-girlfriend, captured and contained

2.

The first time you inhale, I am certain
that you have chosen cocaine over me
a cycle that I will not participate in
I scratch the stamp off the letter I will never send.

3.

I dream a lover in Lebanon.
A bomb drops and we take cabs to Atwater.
I am asked to hold one side of a banner I cannot read.
I hide my face behind it

4.

This is the walk we did for Israel, not knowing.
My brother covets stark Jews Against the Occupation buttons
I remove one from his jacket before he gets on the GO Train.
This is it, not simple, not right, but true.

Drunken Butterfly

1.

I did not know how to tell you I that I researched your birthday,
but I did.

2.

You will never know that this is me:
War waged one country apart.
A song about something else,
anything but young sons drafted,
anything but my family fleeing.
The inevitability of fighting yours means
I cannot look you in the eye.
This modern romance
church basement hardcore of our shared pasts
is noted.

3.

You ask me why I've put up no photos of you,
and my name three times:
I love you, I love you, I love you.

Titles for a Book Told in Photographic Memory

Snapshots Pinned To A String.
Polaroid Love Is Instant Gratification.
Stills From Super-8 And Other Discontinued Formats.
It's The Full-Colour Spreads Of Family Photos That Really Get Me.
High-Gloss Finish, Unexpected Vibrancy.
Photobooths Have Never Looked So Bleak.

Dark Blue Ocean

In your voice
I hear the deepest blue of the ocean.
Cannot fathom why
they decided to name you
a lake.

Trent-Severn

Here is my confession:
I brought a thousand books.
We were only going to a cottage for two days.

I wanted to swim,
but I brought the whole stack,
a meant-to-read-forever list.

Vinyl spins
My baby, she wrote me a letter.
Very few songs make me think of my father.

She was married to a man
whose coat she keeps hanging in the closet
to lend to cold company.
She takes photos of everyone she knows wearing it.
Her sister buys every boyfriend the same gold chain
to track their reactions.

Here I go again on my own,
Service station Whitesnake moves on to
She's my cherry pie.

At the Trent-Severn Waterway, Young Point Local 27,
things I almost buy:
-tiny wooden canoes
-Dolly Dan playing spoons
-real estate maps of Cavendish and Kawartha lakes
-a speedboat
-John Deere baby socks
-Men's t-shirt that says: *Still Crazy After All These Beers*

Over waterway gates littered with
tiny live sardines,
In my mind, we are growing old together,
making big decisions,
grandiose declarations.

Tara-Michelle Ziniuk

Acknowledgements

Halli Villegas and everyone at Tightrope Books.

Sarah Liss for traditions and for bringing your vodka stars to this book.

Romy Ceppetelli for looking at objects and being so awesome to work with.

Kate Morris for forgotten and remembered English. You are a good friend.

Emily Pohl-Weary for her work on the early drafts of these poems.

Richard Vaughan, Chandra Mayor, Jon Paul Fiorentino and Leah Lakshmi Piepzna-Samarasinha for your kind and generous words.

Trish Salah, Hadassah Hill, Johnny Schilling, Daniel Vandervoort, Tania Tabar, Roxanna Vahed, Karlyn Volpe, Ambrose Kirby, Chris Neale, Saira Chhibber, Zoe Whittall, Mattilda Bernstein Sycamore, Maxwell Parrish, Courtney Kelly, Val Sowell, Teresa Giardina, Jaysun Taylor, Siobhan Flood, Katherine Payne, David Findlay, Ryan Hinds, Christopher Hayden, Shala Bennett, Bo Yih Thom, Amanda Dorter, Mark Bialkowski, Shauna Lancit, Jola Sobolak and James Butler—for your continued support and friendship, I am very lucky.

Thank you also to the support of Kiss Machine and the Ontario Arts Council.

Credits:

"You walk like a healthy meal" is a lyric from Califone's Don't Let Me Die Nervous. "You're so pretty when you're faithful to me" is a take on lyrics from The Pixies' Bone Machine. Ussama Abu el-Sheikh quoted from his writing on electronicintifada.net. Numerous poem titles are borrowed song titles, many thanks to their originators.